"After reading 'Surviving the Business of Dying,' I immediately contacted a family friend who is an attorney and got the ball rolling on a will for both my husband and me, so that our children will be cared for in the event of our death. This most critical guide takes you through every step necessary to organize and prepare for the inevitable death of a spouse or loved one. I am grateful to MJ Charles for having the courage and the wherewithal to pen such an extensive guide." **Geri R.**

"Based on personal experience, this book provides non-professional, but heartfelt, advice for managing in the aftermath of a loved one's death in real time through advanced preparation." **Ruth G.**

"MJ has been there and done that. Having gone through the the estate settlement process the hard way, she knows of what she speaks. This is a practical, easy-to-understand guide." **John G.**

"MJ Charles successfully accomplishes two difficult tasks. She both motivates us to think about the practical details we must confront when our spouse dies and very clearly guides us through steps we can now take to make those inevitable jobs more manageable. With her fresh personal experience of loss and smart humor, she leaves us ready to take on these important topics that are so important yet tempting to ignore." **Kristina H.**

"...although this inevitable moment will touch all of our lives, most seem completely disconnected from this actual life event. MJ Charles takes us through a step by step process to prepare. this is our reality checklist." **Dan R.**

Surviving the Business of Dying

A Guide to Why Final Papers Matter

by MJ Charles

In loving memory of my sister Eileen,

who was as excited as I,

when I told her I had a book.

Preface

This story was written three weeks after my husband died. The end was sudden, though he had been ill. We had discussed "things" many times, but nothing was ever put in writing. In the days following the funeral, my brain had so much flying around inside (shock/finality/my business/estate business to name a few), I could barely function. I was left without a map of any kind and no one to ask.

Call it self-preservation, but my old habit of making lists kicked in. I sat in front of a yellow pad with pen in hand and proceeded to empty my brain. Two yellow pads later, my story appeared. Upon review, I decided it was a guide. This guide has been edited over time for redundancy and privacy, but my story remains.

My book evolved from the first-hand experience of learning the hard way each step that awaits you, after the death of a spouse. When a signed Will and accompanying documents are pulled together for the purpose of instructing those who follow in your absence, the shock of your passing is at once diminished by the mere fact there is a plan at hand.

Signed documents confirm your wishes and relieve some of the immense responsibility placed upon the person named to facilitate your affairs in your absence. Your signature represents both your "permission" and authorization for him/her to facilitate what must be done without question or delay.

The time you spend now taking care of your business, as if you were leaving tomorrow, is an enormous gift of the heart. The Will is only one document among many, as you will learn. Get your yellow pad. Begin the conversation. Start the process, if only for yourself. Make lists of all passwords, doctor names, contact information, even a caregiver for your favorite animals or plants! List whatever matters to you.

The purpose of this book is not to scare anyone. We know no one lives forever. Some of us are blessed with longevity; others leave with no notice at all, as my experience shows. Rather, this book is an effort to push you and your spouse to begin this process and finish it.

My hope for this book is to alleviate angst and stress for others. As someone who flew by the seat of her pants, ferreting out what needed to be done, gathering unknown papers from people I barely knew and meeting new people upon whom I had to rely...for eighteen months, I believe the solution is simple. Write it down ahead of time.

Proceed with caution, but most of all proceed! There will still be work to do, but the black hole of ignorance will be plugged. Know you are leaving the best gift of all – instructions!

MJ Charles

CONTENTS

Surviving the Business of Dying

I. Ground Zero

You are on auto-pilot. You have seen movies, read short stories/articles about the moment a spouse dies. The surviving spouse is seen, reflecting on her new life in the dark days after the funeral. Perhaps, you have been a "first responder," along with other family members, helping in any way you can. This is different. This time it is your spouse who died. You are the front line. You are now the widow/widower.

All "helpers" defer to you. This realization makes itself known, as your brain tries to grasp the emotional, the logical and the enormous number of "think-about-it-laters," in its attempt to settle into its new world. People speak to you gently, respectfully, even quietly as if you had open heart surgery. "How are you doing?" rings in your ears. You are receiving constant interruptions and well-meaning suggestions. At the same time, decisions are required in short order. The feeling of being overwhelmed doesn't cover it.

Note: A close friend called me on Day #2 (the day after my spouse died). Nicely, but definitively, he stated "You have a lot of power right now. No one will argue with you. Use it to your advantage." Taken aback at first, I nervously attempted to laugh it off, but he instantly restated himself.

I grabbed this order and decided to take full advantage – if that's the right term - and *manned* this battle station. Moral: In tough times, don't flinch. Just take charge. Everyone else will fall into line. It works.

Consult *your professionals*. Call your closest friends and relatives (they can be friends too) to engage their help. They will make it happen for you. If you don't live near your relatives (I did not), you then will rely upon your friends. These are the very people who have seen you in action before. They will respect your wishes and you will value their insights and suggestions. Assume "mission mode" as you consider the volume of tasks before you that need to be *done in time for the funeral*. List your helpers, assign a task and keep going.

Some background…

Despite all the magazine articles on death and dying, the availability of insurance information, AARP advisories and wellness tips provided in brochures and never-ending life improvement advertising on TV, there remain those individuals who for unknown reasons do not write a Will. They go through life without any kind of medical coverage, die without leaving a signed/witnessed medical directive or any kind of Power-of-Attorney, let alone a Living Will. Bank accounts are held in their name alone. Some have named a beneficiary, but not all.

If you discover such omissions in the days after your spouse's passing, questions will filter through your brain. These sound like, but are not limited to, "Was this an oversight of the bank, when the accounts were first opened?" or "Was it something your spouse held off doing because..." While these questions are natural, their answers - if learned - could be haunting. Do not go there. The answers don't matter now.

Understand out of the gate that these thoughts are gremlins! Do NOT give this type of thinking your time or energy. Reasons for what is in place and what is not can be debated later by others. When you are in the midst of a death aftermath, *there is no debate*. You don't need any distractions. The processing of this immediate moment, that is - planning the funeral and reception - will require every ounce of your inner moxie in order for you to make your way through the morass of it all. Leave your questions for another day in the distant future.

This small book will walk you through the paces of my last three weeks. It is, of course, still unfolding. For the most part, the shock wave has passed. I think. My immediate attempt in writing this is to brief you on the obvious, the not-so-obvious, the sometimes bizarre conversations you might encounter and how I handled them.

Lastly, I will create a list of definitions, a timeline and planning documents for you to fill out for yourself and yes – for your spouse....**now**.

The list of *what-not-to-do* is more or less a venting on my side, since one has to live through this in order to write about the experience cohesively and from the heart. It is cathartic to write about one's woes, but I don't think I will take this tack. This approach is self-serving and would no doubt lead to a bored reader, defeating the book's purpose. The reflections on the past 21 days will hopefully make the way straighter, less emotional (when it comes to money) and make sense to anyone reading of such things for the first time.

It is my personal conclusion that the less critical thinking one is required to do immediately after this particular life-shifting event, the less strain there is on *your* health. You need a map. I call it a guide.

II. Documentation

Think of an old map. It sits crinkled, maybe weather stained, with arrows pointing "N, E, W, S" (Yes, it spells NEWS.) These torn, yellow sheets guided explorers to a safe port with pictures of islands, trees and an "X" at their hopeful destination. Although this type of map might also remind one of a "treasure hunt," this is not my intent here. There should be no "hunt." Rather, there should be one place where a brightly colored binder is kept for easy access, in case of need, with the following list of documents:

1. A Will

2. A Living Will (different from the above)

3. Legal Power-of-Attorney

4. Medical Directive for your state

5. Medical Power of Attorney (separate from any other Power of Attorney)

6. List of bank accounts – both personal and business

7. Bank branch locations/bank contacts

8. List of investments, any contact name and their phone numbers

9. List of all passwords associated with bank accounts

10. List of computer passwords, email passwords, any   social media passwords

11. Business records, a partnership agreement, EIN (Employer Identification Number)

12. List of any other assets

13. Copies of tax returns – both personal & business-like

14. Names and phone numbers for your attorney, tax person, accountant (if different from tax person), financial planner (if you have one. One is highly recommended.), etc.

15. Social Security numbers for you and your spouse

16. List of bills paid online with due dates/ amounts and passwords

If you co-own a company, try to keep a list of meeting dates with business partner(s) that you attended with your spouse at various times. This allows you credibility, when/if business monies come into probate conversations later.

The list is not a legal document, but can be used as a reminder to the partner, if asked about joint accounts or if any money is owed to the now deceased partner.

> **Note**: My list of documents is to *start* the process for you. It is not deemed to be complete and the list will vary person to person. *Just begin.*

The whole point of this exercise is that you have a map for your survivors! If you wind up as the surviving spouse, you will find answers to all questions that will be asked of you. Attorneys, doctors, funeral directors and heirs have very different needs. You are now the point person, trying to answer any and all questions quickly and easily with the least amount of stress (for you!) possible. *This is in the first week.*

Think of your own wishes. It is much easier to read a prepared statement, rather than wonder what someone would want for you and/or others... albeit, in a hurry. This project takes time to gather and assemble (colored folders for simple organization), but once compiled, it is a huge gift, both to receive and leave behind. I call it "consideration."

Having a Will is the single most important legal piece of this after-the-fact human puzzle. Its origination and composition is well worth the investment of a *probate* attorney (one who deals with wills almost exclusively), so nothing is left out or remains open for interpretation later.

Unless there is significant prior planning, both financially and legally, if the assets are over a certain amount set by your state (varies from state-to-state), *you will need an attorney* whether you have a Will or not. Having met your attorney before a crisis arrives, and hearing him/her greet you by name when you are, is at the very least helpful.

This person is already familiar with your estate and understands the hows and whys it came to be. Leave it to them to answer any questions. A well written Will eliminates all guesswork in your absence and precludes the less-than-random thought of "attorney shopping" in the week following the funeral.

This last thought is a bizarre exercise. Attorney-shopping usurps energy from your inner being at a time when it is needed inside you just to maintain. Its price is exacted *upon your physical and emotional health.* Like any other last minute "investment shopping," you will make mistakes. Figure it as too expensive and start your attorney search today.

In a perfect world, the Will is drawn up before any crisis with forethought and deliberation. It will have been signed by the "decedent," witnessed and in some states, notarized. These last two details vary state-to-state. I would share a few general points:

1. There should be more than one copy of a signed Will. The original (usually) goes home with you to be kept in a safe or safety deposit box. This place should be known by your spouse and executor* (if different people) so they know where to find it, *when necessary.*

   Your attorney will have a copy and/or your executor*. (*An executor is the person whom you have chosen to carry out or "execute" your wishes, as directed in your Will. "Executrix" is the female version of this word.)

2. The copy does *not* have legal authority. Ensure that the original is accessible to the executor.

NOTE: Remember, after hearing/witnessing the news that your spouse has passed, you will be on autopilot. You will have been sucker punched, even if you saw the end coming. Your brain is operating on a different level. Simple recall will not be a reliable trait. *You will need others to remember things.*

3. *Have both Wills done at the same time.* You want to leave your own instructions for when/if you can't speak for yourself. You want your wishes known as to what to do or NOT at your own funeral, who should care for your animals, etc. Think of as many details as possible and keep your notes in the same file.

4. It is the sane, practical, frugal, intelligent and considerate thing to do.

III.   Not a Leg To Stand On

If there is no Will .. there is an entirely different process.   This process starts literally the day after your spouse dies.   Wait until after the funeral to make some phone calls, but start making a list of all pertinent questions in any case.

Write down things as they come to mind. You can formulate a plan and "triage" by immediacy later. You will need an attorney, in particular a "probate" attorney, if your late spouse:

> 1. held assets exceeding a certain total (varies state-to-state);

> 2. had heirs (in addition to you), including children, stepchildren and grandchildren, to name a few;

> 3. owned a business of his own and/or has a business partner;

> 4. held assets that are not also in your name and a variety of reasons more.

Ask a few trusted people for a referral. Know ahead of time you MUST like your attorney, so it might take more than one phone call. If your spouse dies mid-week, your first appointment might be well into the next week. That could fall on the day of the funeral. The next day is "get away day" for that attorney. This puts you two week out and so it goes. Eliminate the wait, ask a friend begin the process for you.

Estates without a will are overseen by the decedent's "personal representative," instead of an executor. This is the case in my state. It can vary, so be sure to check what happens where you live.

Since the deceased did not write a Will, there is no one named as an executor to take care of unfinished business or facilitate asset disbursement, if any, among heirs. This is where state law (varies) kicks in.

A personal representative is customarily the surviving spouse, though the role can be passed to the oldest adult child or close family member. While some people feel they are up to the task, the fiduciary (trust in you on behalf of others) responsibilities entailed by this bonded legal position can quickly become a second job.

I strongly recommend hiring an attorney to wade through the process with you. Just the registration required to obtain court papers certifying you as "Personal Representative" can be cumbersome and time consuming, if not done properly. Meanwhile, "time is of the essence" is ringing in your ears. No one can learn *fast,* especially in times of undue stress.

There are exceptions to this last paragraph, namely - if you are familiar with the law or have few assets and/or heirs. It is rocky territory, however, to go it alone.

Bank accounts are "frozen," unless you were already a co-signor on an account. If you are not on the account, the bank freezes all monies. This means no money can be taken out of the account until you can prove you represent the "Estate of..."

In this case, the bank requires you to present your state-issued personal representative certificate. This certificate proves you are bonded and the state probate court recognizes you as the person who will facilitate the deceased's affairs.

This must happen before any money is moved. When the money is withdrawn from the decedent's accounts, the funds are then deposited in the soon-to-be opened estate bank account. This account "houses" the money until probate closes several months from now or the attorney says otherwise.

Again, rules differ from state to state. This credential arrives approximately 2 weeks after the legal request is filed with the probate court. Know ahead of time you are your own advocate. If your papers do not arrive in ten days, call the attorney to confirm all forms were sent to the courts and if so, when.

Start a log in an old fashioned copybook or in excel. Record the date/time and reason for your call. This log becomes your "memory bank," allowing you to track the reliability of the attorney office as you proceed. There is little you can do to push this along, but your interest will be duly noted. Lastly, make sure you are not invoiced by the attorney for requiring an update.

If there are heirs, you will need all current addresses of the heirs (in addition to you), their birth dates and social security numbers. These are required for future court proceedings and documents.

If there are minors, i.e. grandchildren, you may be asked to act as custodian for their inheritance until they are 18 years old. Alternatively, the probate court might appoint an "attorney ad litem" instead. This court-appointed attorney represents minors, so that they in fact receive their fair share of any estate distribution due to them. This attorney works hand-in-hand with the personal representative as the probate process continues. You will need the minors' full legal names, their social security numbers and street addresses for court papers.

Start making a list of all assets, including real estate, partnership agreements, bank accounts, investment accounts and anything else of value. Make notes next to each, if it is held in common or already has a designated beneficiary and when it was acquired. This list becomes "the estate inventory" and will be included in court papers.

If you are meeting an attorney and his/her paralegal (assistant), you will receive detailed instructions – kindly issued - to fully grasp and put into action "in an effort to expedite matters." If you do not understand this important, detailed information, make that known.

Ask these almost complete strangers, in whose hands your fate now rests, to repeat and explain their requests in simpler terms, so you will understand. Also, ask for a timeline of probate events of some sort now (at the beginning), so you know what's coming down the pike ahead of time. Having an attorney-issued list of probate needs will lessen the stress of each stage. You will be ready for it.

It has been my observation that some people are too enamored by their own knowledge to gauge their client's absorption level. It is the professional's tendency to speak in "industry jargon," leaving the audience to wonder. While this display is considered rude or presumptuous in a social setting, stilted rhetoric is useless, especially when one is in need and requires knowledge. It is in fact not fair and too important to miss.

Don't be overly impressed or intimidated because you are in a law firm. Unless or until you have received all your answers in a way you understand them, ask. You are a smart person; you will learn what you need to know and you will get the job done.

This is an overwhelming experience all by itself and can be debilitating. Cry the frustration away all the way home if you have to, but complete your question list. Ask as many repetitive questions and their follow-ups as you need to in order to nail down what is required. Remember "the power?" Take charge (in your brain). Remember you are new to this and to them. You have an immense respon-sibility to perform and want to get it right. Lastly, you are paying them to make you aware of how to move.

Be firm. Be professional, but do ask yet again "What was that?" "How does that work? I want to understand this." "Could you say that again, please, in another way. I want to get it right." Last but not least, don't apologize.

Attorneys and their assistants do this for a living. Everyone is in a rush, but it is incumbent upon them to make sure:

    a.   They have all they need to get the job done;

    b.   You have the information you need - and understand why – in order to get this job done. You might have to remind them you really are on the same side!

Investment bankers, if any, factor into this rush. The investment banker will be a "team member," as time goes on. This person should be on your "Notify List" for after the funeral.

Once the Personal Representative papers arrive, you will meet with this person to set up the transfer of assets into the estate account, if there is no beneficiary listed on the account. If there is a beneficiary name, this money is then given to that person directly, as it is considered "out of estate." Keep in mind, even bankers are "vendors." As professionals, they will listen and be helpful.

At the same time, this banker's incentive is to keep the monies *in their bank*. Their long term hope is that you will keep your inheritance (if there is one) with them, rather than move your money to another bank.

Don't make this decision now, even if you are asked. Just keep it in the back of your head for the day when disbursements are made and the estate is closed.

Do not "invest your share" prior to any final court proclamation You could easily find yourself in an unwanted situation if you do. As Personal Representative, you have a "fiduciary responsibility" (the court's trust in you on behalf of others) to care for this money until the probate judge signs the completion papers several months away. The monies might be shared with you eventually (no promises), but until it has gone through the probate process, all of the decedent money and investments stay in the estate account.

I was asked to "move the money for investment purposes" several months prior to close of probate. I was speechless. From my own banking background, I thought the request was at once premature and very presumptuous. I had yet to discuss any of my possible future plans with this banker. I would not have known them if he asked! Let's just say my tone changed. I let him know I took issue with this request, simply stating it wasn't happening. I used "my power."

Remember, these people are players on what is becoming "your team." They are working on your behalf. You will need to speak with your team until the probate process is completed sometime in the next 8-18 months and funds have been disbursed. Remain civil and keep going.

> **Note**: Upon introduction, if an attorney does not give you his/her absolute respect, make it a short meeting. For example, if you receive fleeting eye contact, as they defer to someone else in the meeting or if they do not listen, while you are speaking, stop talking. Do not hire inattention.

In my first meeting, I was ushered into a meeting with an attorney by well-meaning family members. This man proceeded to speak to *them*, mispronounced my name and never asked what state *I lived in*. My brain was in a thick fog, as my husband had died only 21 hours prior. I really don't know what this man said, but my brain heard *how* he said it. Whether it was a matter of too much too soon or self preservation, I ended the meeting with "Thank you for this. That will be it for now."

My ears resounded with "the sooner, the better," as I left the law firm behind. There was a handshake from a man whom I had never met before with "profoundly sorry for your loss" bouncing around in my head from someone I had just resolved to never see again.

"Thank you's" were spoken as I walked out the door. I quickly got into the car shell-shocked. I thanked the family member, but stated I would find my own attorney. I returned home to stare out the window. The day was mind-blowing.

     Lesson: Get through the funeral first! Do NOT rush to an attorney whom you do not know, even if "it is highly recommended" by a distant relative. Make a couple of calls to your sources (close friends or even business associates) to find attorney names; let them start making calls for probate attorneys. But don't you start this process until after the funeral. It is a project unto itself. You already have several right in front of you.

     <u>Good News</u>! *You can skip this previous section!* Starting with "If there is no Will…".   *IF* you get your wills done *NOW*.

     At this point in my guide, let's take a breath. Find a different spot to sit and clear your brain.

I never liked roller coasters. When I found myself on one – whether to placate a date or my son, when he was young – I would close my eyes, shut up and wait for the car to pull into the station. So it is in times like this. Sit down, buckle up and hang on. This ride will end of its own accord. It is not in our control one way or the other. Go through the motions. Get through the day. Keep a schedule of sorts – eating when you usually do and sleeping as often as possible. You need the rest.

Another analogy for the days building up to the funeral is that of an impending storm. Just this week, the National Hurricane Center made it known that they are predicting a limited numbers of storms for summer 2015 (only 2-3). The article continues, "Certain parts of the southeastern and northeastern United States are way overdue *for a large storm.*" Most of the people who live in these areas are young enough that they did not live through "the big storms" of the '40s, '50s or '60s. In effect, no one understands what to do or why. They are more apt to have a "hurricane party," than board up and drive inland. It is called preparation. They don't do it and we read about them the next day. So it is with Wills and lists. It is time to prepare for your personal big storm. Do it now.

Returning to "Surviving the Business of Dying"

IV. The Hospital

The ambulance ride took him to the ER, where he was "worked on." They then brought him (your loved one) up to the Intensive Care Unit, or "ICU," as care and tests continued. At the same time, the reception room became a busy place, as conversation ran the gambit of sudden life changes to death documents to finding tea.

In the last four hours, you have *made friends* with the staff and seemingly, they with you. They have tended to your family and spouse and are genuinely concerned about you. In-laws arrive; phones are in action.

The Will conversation (Reference Picture, Page 8) rises – "Is there a Will?" Inquiries come up, seemingly as easy daily conversation. There is a momentary thought of "That's intrusive!" answered with a strong "I don't think so." These headlines are fleeting, as more people arrive. Time has no measurement.

Then, the doctor appears. Chatter ceases, as he sits next to you. He professionally, yet definitively, asks "Do you have any papers?" This is the moment you should hand him your spouse's medical directive. (Note: Each state has its medical directive online.) Like the movies, all eyes are on you. In my case, there was not a signed medical directive to present. Providence, however, had stepped in to solve this dilemma.

Earlier that morning, I tried to persuade my husband again to sign a medical directive. As I sat on the ottoman in front of him with the directive in my lap, I realized I could record his medical directive. I asked his permission (recording this as well), to which he agreed. At 8:00 am, I read the state medical directive word-by-word, with as little emotional conviction as I could muster. Unbeknownst to me, I would need this proof later that same day.

In reading the state medical directive, I stopped at the end of each paragraph, asking the stated questions in a "Yes" or "No" manner. I also verified each step of the way as to whether or not he understood. He would then nod in agreement or shake his head "no."

It took eight minutes, but I had it.

Fast forward to 4:00 pm that afternoon. We (my son, stepson, brother-in-law, the business partner and I) were in the reception room. With the doctor next to me, I explained the above. He was amazed, as he had never been presented with something like this before. In fact, he appreciated having the video, as it allowed him to hear, see and in part, confirm the physical and mental condition of his patient. He heard the patient in his own words and at that point stated, "I have my marching orders." There was no question as to the wishes of my spouse. A priest had already been called; my husband would be disconnected from his breathing apparatus and would die shortly after.

The nurse, who just an hour earlier escorted me through the ICU and into his room, requested my presence in the hall. Quietly, she asked "What funeral home were you thinking of?" Was I thinking of a funeral home?

I rode home in a stupor of sorts with my son at my side. We said little. We were both in shock after the last few hours. The plan for the next five days was going to be survivor mode, namely - eat/sleep/get up /get dressed, proceed. A veritable "Let the games begin" took over.

The illness is over; your what-ifs are relieved. Now there is a new game clock running. Ready? Start.

V. Funeral Plans

Self is # 1. You must care for yourself. Remember this. Try not to make too many decisions too fast; let others help. Bring a mature (stable, centered) family member - hopefully, someone who has run this route before - with you to the funeral home and the church. You will be making all the plans for the coming week. Though you will be present in body, your mind will drift. It is good to have a second pairs of ears to grasp all the details and requested timelines.

Note: It is a well-known fact that in times of high stress people revert to their native tongue. In my case, "my tongue" is New York with Irish influence. My rhetorical style is my way of coping, somewhat frank with a slice of humor. Even if you think you've got it together, rest assured - you do not. You will say things that might be shocking, ill-timed, etc. So please: A. Don't worry about it and B. If someone else does, just move on. Say a prayer that they will never know what you are feeling in this moment.

Try to find a local funeral home. The one-to-one "let me help" approach is still in place. This meeting is a drill, so go well fed and ready to do business. Decisions on destinations/timing/pallbearers, choice of burial or cremation and items you never thought of are made quickly, as you are guided by those who do this for a living. To their credit I found it long, but relatively uneventful. The receptionist even shared the same name as my mother. I took it as a "sign." As it turned out, a family member and I worked with an employee who, once upon a time, had worked for the original owners of the funeral home. Every possible courtesy was extended to us in order to accomplish this immense task and make it as seamless as possible.

Most family-owned funeral homes today have been sold and are run by nationwide corporations. While you are sitting in well-designed meeting rooms, funeral home assistants are now basically sales reps, who might be visited by a regional sales manager during your session. This scene ensures you *know everything that is available to you.* It's quite the sales experience.

For instance, did you know there are funeral DVDs, "thumb print" jewelry and after-care therapy! Guest books for $85+ and candles with your decedent's picture wrapped around them are optional. Mints wrapped in the company logo complete the sales items. Lastly, there is bunco night for surviving spouses. (This invitation comes in the mail shortly after the funeral.)

As I sat there listening to the regional sales manager in plaid pants, my mind drifted. Survivor humor prevailed. All I could think of was Chevy Chase! It was time for him to pop out and yell "LIVE FROM PORTLAND! IT'S …." But I digress.

Among the funeral details is a very important *business* item that requires your attention. This is the death certificate. *It is the first document you need, whether you are the executor or going to be the personal representative.*

The death certificate accompanies your application for the Certificate of Personal Representative (or that of Executor) and will be required, in addition to the certificate, as proof of your authority with regard the deceased's estate.

The funeral home takes care of the death certificate for you, but it is good to know about ahead of time. Be sure to order several copies, at least three long and three short. This is not a state requirement, but a reminder to order several copies, so you have enough to give to banks, utilities, etc., if you are asked for them. It takes anywhere from 5-10 days to obtain, depending on your county. You can also go to your county health department yourself to pick these up, instead of waiting for the funeral home. It might be faster.

Traditions and cost considerations differ from family to family, region to region. There might be a wake, newspaper obituaries, a private service or not. The choice is yours. If you are attending and begin to wonder "Why didn't they...," leave your questions on the doorstep. Time and money are well in place in the business of funerals.

Religion

Religion can be a consideration at the time of a funeral. Any religion – traditional, eastern or new wave - allows for already established formats, prayers and blessings. This is hugely appreciated by the living at this time.

Since most funerals occur within days after the death, the format, prayer/ blessing selections and music options are handed to you by a priest/rabbi/minister/ facilitator. These predetermined programs remove another weight off your shoulders. You cannot figure it all out by yourself and make it to the funeral in time. Rather, review the suggestions, check off those that mean the most *to you* and return it to the source. They will take it from there. Mark it "Done" and move down your list.

As tasks appear, ask a *competent* friend or an older child to be your "secretary." It is this person who can find and assign other "jobs" for the funeral, i.e. pall bearers, readers, speakers. Helpful hint: This new "right hand" can type individual readings into WORD, then email the pieces to the individuals who will be reading at the ceremony. Everyone needs to rehearse.

Delegating tasks is not only necessary to save time, but is also medicinal for you. Competent people, *including children, are waiting to be asked.* They *need* to help. It is their gift at a special time and is why you have them! Ask your newly appointed secretary to make note of each name and "their job." These names should then be added to the thank you list and included in the funeral program for recognition. The program is given to guests, as they leave the service.

While "relax" is not quite the word for this moment, you can take stock that all items are being handled and these people can get the job done. Keep crossing things off your list as you assign them. A short list is a good thing.

I called upon my former parish as the venue for my husband's funeral. To my surprise, three ladies with whom I had worked on school committees "in the day" were still there. I received hugs, tears and flowers. Without another word, Karen did the flowers; Roseann sang and Jane made the picture displays for the reception. Done, done and done! I heard familiar voices – welcoming tones – and knew these items were well in hand.

If you have not been to church /temple in a long time, this makes NO difference in times such as a death. You will be amazed how helpful and sincere and loving people will be. They will, quite literally, come to your rescue. It is one of those human things that people do for other people. Know this and believe this. Caveat? Be ready to do this for someone else. No questions asked; just show up and make it happen.

The family dynamic is the antithesis to that of organized religion. A list of jobs can be composed for family members who wish to participate in the ceremony. Try to delegate this duty as well, and be sure to include the children. *Anyone* who can read is eligible. It teaches all that inclusion, confidence and love are still part of the family framework.

Eulogies

Know ahead of time that you will have volunteers. "I am giving the eulogy," says a family member. Sometimes, a gulp is in order.

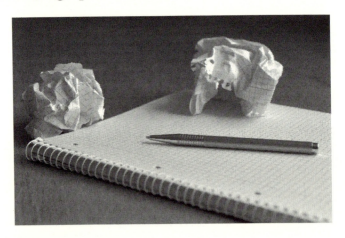

Set parameters

The eulogy is one task that the spouse should have some input, so the day of the funeral is dignified and not an impromptu showcase theater. In keeping with rules of a good speech teacher, be sure to issue a time limit, i.e. three to five minutes. If there is more than one speaker, the time limit lowers to three to four minutes.

For timid speakers, intercede with suggested topics and/or pointers, i.e. no historical perspective. Dates/names/places are boring and could require confirmation. Given time constraints, confirmation might not be possible. The speaker could get confused, losing focus on what his/her point really is.

Rather, use the speech formula of old, namely - pick three points that *the deceased held dear.* Add two to three sentences for each point and close. Amen. That is three to five minutes. Stories – funny ones – are great "filler" and allow the audience/congregation to know a little bit more about your spouse. Laughs are a useful grief "tool" and welcomed by the masses. Remember, adhere to time limits, if there is more than one speaker. Nothing is worse than a long funeral!

In my case, it took the speaker nearly five days to create his eulogy. It was a tense time for the whole family, as he ascended the steps to the microphone. Clear voiced, on point, composed 95% of the time – he did one heck of job. He nailed it! Those in the front bench could allow their shoulders to relax, no doubt in relief after all the drama, but he did a great job. Sometimes, you just gotta believe.

Reception

Most often, the funeral is followed by a reception. It is the one time that family, neighbors, business friends and school chums, many of whom have traveled a distance to get there, can share some time together. What foods are served and how long the gathering will be varies from tradition to tradition. Again, most churches, temples/mosques or community centers have reception areas, where families can meet with old friends. Funeral attendees are welcomed and are free to visit at will, re-establishing life-long ties and shared memories.

"Church ladies" are on hand to set up and place the flowers. The buffet is quickly arranged, as food arrives via caterer or neighbors. You arrive at a well-planned, ready-for-company event. Accept the day, as a gift from those who care – even if you don't know them. You are then free to genuinely visit and, yes, take a breath.

Note: Don't forget to eat! All this action (funeral and reception) usually happens in one day. Your emotional well-being requires sustenance because your body will forget to mention it. Get in line, take a plate, visit as you go, but eat.

As you speak with people, understand that their recommendations and suggestions are expressed with love from the bottom of their hearts. What you remember afterward can be entertaining. For instance, three very different (age/style/walk of life) women told me at various times during the reception in their whispered voices -

"Now you can put your furniture where you want it!" Oh my goodness! Just keep moving, thanking, meeting, greeting, sometimes eating - - and know they need this as much as you do. Nothing goes unnoticed.

Note: Wear comfortable shoes. You will be standing... a lot.

Receptions are also commonly held at a family member's home or a favorite restaurant of the deceased. It is all a matter of tradition and financial consideration.

VI. The Aftermath

The funeral and reception are now over. Exhaustion is an understatement. Once home, you find your favorite chair and sit for a long moment. What the hell just happened? Life of one week ago is gone forever – be it good or bad. It is over.

Your questions will take weeks or months to answer or be absorbed into oblivion, as your brain unloads. Keep life simple. When family leaves and your house is full of flowers, enjoy them. Use every vase you own. Go for walks. If you don't have a dog, ask a neighbor if you can walk their dog. This time is yours.

Neighbors are wonderful people! They are ready and willing to help, visit, show up and go home! I was included in an old fashioned Italian backyard dinner four days after the funeral.

I sat with this wonderful, multi-generational family for only two hours, but the conversation and the companionship was at once supportive, endearing and very much needed. Once seated with their over-sized yellow Labrador Retriever's head on my lap, my pasta was served to me in a bowl. "Mom" handed me the warm bread basket and someone refilled my wine glass without hesitation. I cried as I walked home, but for a whole new reason. I knew I was going to be OK.

Self Care and Social Contact

The three most important points here are all free. They are: sleep, walk and time. Self care might be a new undertaking all by itself. So be it. You are *in a new world.*

Gently, calmly, begin feeling well, fit and rested. You need not talk about this plan of yours. It is between you and yourself. Once you practice this, it becomes an intricate element of your inner strength.

Then you can take care of everything else. Don't forget your power. It should be part of you by now. There is no reason to give it up whatsoever. People listened to you in the last few weeks. You will want them to hear you as time goes on. You are in charge of you. Trust this.

You have received a major body blow - albeit emotionally- but we know unanswered emotional distress can be devastating to us physically over time. You couldn't take time to be alone before because of your caregiver role along that of breadwinner or however your life was before. Now you *must* take time to do just this. Cooperate with the healing process and you will be OK. Ignore it and you will have problems. Maybe not right away, but who wants them at all?

Sleep whenever you can in the days following the funeral. Odd naps work just as well as a good night's sleep, if that is what your body is telling you. Always have a bedtime. Sip tea, go for walks and even talk to strangers. Everything is healing inside and out. Sleep is your friend.

I walk a lot in general, but in the last three weeks my walks were shorter and more frequent. I had my dog with me, so I wasn't lonely, but I am still a social person. On one walk, I took the picture of a grandmother with her granddaughter as they were eating ice cream on a park bench. They were so cute and happy being there. Each greeted me with ice cream all over her face. Smiling, I asked for the grandmother's phone, and she readily handed it over. They smiled their ice cream smiles. Now, they have a picture of their day in the park!

They might think they received a surprise, but I received a gift as well. It warmed my soul this day to see there was "happy" so close to home. A quick picture was just enough "social contact" for one day. I knew I couldn't just sit and gab. First, it would be strange, but more importantly, I couldn't handle it. I had too much emotion flying around in my head!

So, this is all part of it… Know ahead of time, you will be a mess. If you are not a mess, then it is time to make another kind of appointment!

There is no contest winner for "holding in" the most poignant feeling of loss. You glowed when you were in love and certainly (hopefully) when you were married. The indescribable sense of loss appears on your face and speaks volumes in body language without any help. Space your visits with "company." Separate your close friends from "the nosies."

Make short those phone calls that are seemingly well intended on the outset but become invasive. You do not have to give any reason. Just say you are tired and must go. The "curiosity seekers" will care less and probably will not call again anyhow. Understand *you are very tired*, even if you don't feel it. Power time! Be nice, but end the call.

Establish a new schedule for yourself or get back on a schedule, whichever will ease your brain. Your brain needs quiet time to unravel the angst, frustration and sometimes anger toward your deceased loved one. Anger? You bet. Yell at him/her!

Get their picture and talk your heart out – say all that you decided "It wasn't a good time to bring up" in the prior six months. Get it out. Cry, take a long shower and go for another walk. Movies are also good.

Eat well. Do not lie in bed, skip breakfast or any other meal. There is an enormous amount of energy that goes into the aftermath of witnessing an illness or sudden life event. Recovering from a trauma, i.e. the death of a spouse, is akin to recuperation of any other kind. The sick person is gone. It is your time to find that person in the mirror and care for her. You are here and need to be well! Eat what you want, when you want it. Eat healthily, but eat. Take-out works very well.

Sleep. Did I mention this? It is free, healing and an absolute necessity because your brain is exhausted, your body is wiped out and your soul is sad. You will rarely enjoy such a luxury.

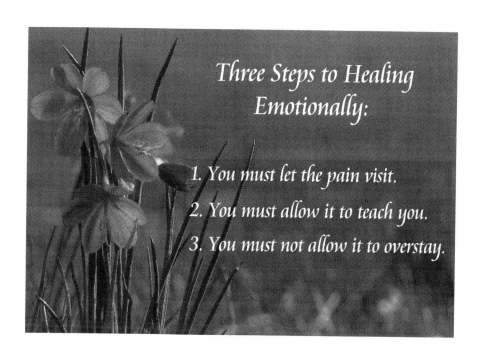

Three Steps to Healing Emotionally:

1. *You must let the pain visit.*
2. *You must allow it to teach you.*
3. *You must not allow it to overstay.*

VII. The World Goes On

At this point, it is my obligation to note here that even though your world has had a seismic shift in the last month, *the rest of the world continued.* Bills must be paid on time – rent, utilities. "How did he pay the phone bill?" will resound in your brain. Automatic payments? Such is life. It continues. It is also "normalcy." It is very okay to know you can still pay bills. It is a task that requires completion. What was once routine can present itself as an enormous project.

Be angry, if the bill paying process is not mapped out. Anger is a welcomed, *required* and very healing emotion! There are just so many tears a person has... do not give them up to bills! Pick one bill. If you know how to pay, pay it. Then, the next. If you don't know this one, put it down. Call the vendor, if you must. Explain the last two weeks. Tell them payment will be coming, as soon as this is all sorted. It's a phone call, but get it done. And put the file away until tomorrow. You did two bills! That's enough for a first try.

Acquire "mission mode" attitude. (Remember, your *power* right now. Use it.) Move on down the seemingly never ending list of things. The chaos does end. Know ahead of time that it is OK, if you goof and you call a few people twice... or not at all! Blame it all on "your state of mind." Who cares? They are pleased you are thinking of them!

Note: This *power* is self-sustaining. In retrospect, each time I used my "new power," I was unknowingly building a new mind muscle. This personal new strength is now muscle memory. Know you will come out of this life phase stronger and more able than ever before. Truth be known, you always had this strength. It's a matter of believing in yourself.

To minimize being overwhelmed, get organized for the upcoming invasion of the "business of dying." Visit the Dollar Store for brightly colored folders, pens and yellow pads. Make a list on a bright paper with a column that says "DONE". Check it off as you go, so you don't have to think about it again.

Odd Notes

The conversation of whether to bury or cremate is many times dictated by one's spiritual or local cultural norms. Cremation has become more common in the West, and in the U.S. in particular, as the "business of dying" is so expensive and land is dwindling. Environmental concerns figure in for some as well. Having said this, if you are not accustomed to the practice of cremation and spreading someone's ashes, it can be disconcerting.

If cremation is decided upon, the finality of leaving the cemetery the same day as the service is not available to you, the mourner. You will speak with the funeral home in perhaps another week, when you are summoned to "pick up the urn." You are barely recovering from the week before and you realize "it" isn't over yet.

In my case, my husband was cremated after the church service. One week later, I was having struts installed into my car, when I received the call. Dressed in khakis and a sweater, while writing thank you notes in a waiting room, my phone rang - "The urn is ready for you." A bit jolted, I thanked the lady and agreed to be there shortly.

Having never participated in this particular exercise before, I needed to center myself. The mechanic let me know the car was ready. I made a stop at McDonald's for comfort food. While inhaling my lunch, the thought occurred to me that this "fast food fix" was highly appropriate. My late husband would many times make this stop on his way home, as evidenced by poorly hidden garbage(!).

With this less-than-reverend thought in mind, I was able to enter the funeral home composed and business-like to retrieve his urn. I was escorted into a dimly lighted "living room" that had two large chairs, a coffee table with a complimentary burning candle with his picture on it alongside of the urn. A deep-voiced man ("Mr. Plaid Pants") asked me if I wanted to sit and spend some time alone. I did not!

I picked up the urn (which was heavy to the point I almost dropped it) and thanked him, as I unceremoniously walked out the double doors. He followed me to the car in his weird caring way, when I opened the car door to the overwhelming scent of McD's fries! I pushed the wrappings out of the way and placed the urn on the seat. Clearly I was annoyed that there were no instructions left regarding this... or anything else.

As you and your spouse consider your ultimate options, be certain to think of those who will be the ones to carry out your instructions. Choosing cremation is only the first step; step two is where the ashes are to be scattered or buried! Talk between yourselves, but also make it known to someone! My suggestion is to choose whichever is the least traumatic for the *surviving spouse*. It will be an immense help at such a time.

Note: In addition to anger or sadness, humor is an extremely relevant and healthy coping "tool." Well-placed humor is at once freeing, disarming and logically shareable. Lastly, it places the soul in a hopeful place. Tendered with timing, it allows you to laugh and the rest will follow.

Finally - "Under the radar" is a term used many times with reference to someone who is avoiding the government, family, etc. After you lose a loved one, you do not own the energy to bounce back into the regular flow of life right away. To do so, denies your spirit the time to heal or to understand all that has happened to you and your family in the preceding week.

Under the radar in this instance is comforting, timely and for most concerned, expected. Most importantly, it is the individual (you) who decides where, when, with whom, for how long you will venture into "normalcy." There is after all a new normal.

One-on-one visits are good with those whom you hold dear. This is not a time for networking, so to speak. If anyone else thinks otherwise, give them "a wide berth," as my mother would say. You do not need to explain yourself and you do not have to endure. If the above fails, just send them to me!

I'm not cutting this short. It is just the end of what I can relay to you right now. Let me know if you have any questions. I am not a psychologist or a psychiatrist, pastor or soothsayer. I am a woman who lost her husband three weeks ago. He had been sick, but the end is always a shock.

My hope is that this guide helps someone (man or woman) to avoid some of the untoward emotion left in the wake of a spouse's sudden death – especially if they leave *intestate* - that is, without a Will. It is okay to go up and come down again in this roller coaster ride of life. The unforeseen twists and turns of this coaster ride make themselves known in a short period of time. The same period of time that is filled with deadlines. This is what rocks your world.

Be good to yourself, if you are at the beginning of this process. Be considerate of those who will have to continue after you are gone. I am still at the beginning of my journey, but I am on my way.

VIII. Two Years After

This life-shifting experience came to its legal closure a few months ago with the probate court filing of "The Completion of Probate for the Estate of...," duly signed and dated by the probate attorney. It took eighteen months, two changes of attorneys (and searches for three), along with never-ending fact checking, questioning and follow-up to ensure all was proper, understood and correct.

Know ahead of time that the probate process does take time in the best of settings, i.e. completed documentation, familiarity with the probate attorney and confidence that all is in order. You can easily bypass much of the angst, frustration and not-knowing, however, if you "use your power" to start making your list today. Your ear becomes attuned to attorney names, which should be your first stop.

No doubt, there is a learning curve for whomever is named an executor. When the day arrives, that person will have to call upon every managerial and administrative skill they have gleaned in their adult life. Even if they have held such jobs professionally, the difference between the two is emotion. This "job" is not for one's advancement. Rather, it is a trust bestowed upon one person by another (either the state or the deceased) for the benefit of others related by blood.

You will not, however, have to shop for an attorney, search for documents, if they exist - or wonder aloud "what would (deceased person) do?" I hope you use "your power" now. Start this task. Include your spouse/partner to the degree they cooperate, but get yours done. It will be your guide for those who remain after you are gone. Your Will is a piece of this pie; other pieces are part of your Will.

The result is a single notebook, professionally prepared, containing your wishes and instructions in one place. Take stock in that you have left your very best effort for those whom you love most.

MJ Charles

Definitions
(Not a complete list of documents)

Advanced Medical Directive: A legal document (*also known as a Living Will*) signed by a competent person to provide guidance for medical and health-care decisions (such as the termination of life support or organ donation) in the event the person becomes incompetent to make such decisions.

Attorney Ad Litem: An attorney appointed by a court to act as an advocate for a minor, a proposed ward, or unknown heirs in a particular legal action (such as a divorce). This person is part of the estate process; your probate attorney decides if this is needed and will make appropriate contacts. No need to find one on your own.

COD: Cause of Death, as stated on the official death certificate.

Death Certificate: Legal document signed by the doctor/medical examiner and verified by the funeral home director, stating date and cause. It is then filed with the county or state department of records. Required document to facilitate deceased's financial and personal business.

EIN: Employer Identification Number required by the Internal Revenue Service for estate bank account(s); essential for filing estate tax return. Obtained from the IRS; call information and make request. An official letter will be sent to the executor, stating the estate EIN.

Executor/Executrix: The person named in a will as the person who will make sure that the instructions in the will are properly followed.

Financial Planner or Advisor: There two kinds of financial planners. Some financial planners advise clients in their money management only. Other financial planners must pass their state FINRA Series 6 and FINRA 7 exams in order to obtain a . license to buy and sell securities on behalf of their clients.

ICU: Intensive Care Unit is a separate section of a hospital, where the critically ill are cared for.

Living Will: A document in which the signer requests to be allowed to die rather than be kept alive by artificial means if disabled beyond a reasonable expectation of recovery.

Medical Power-of-Attorney: In the most basic form, a *health care power of attorney* merely says, "I want this person to make decisions about my health care if I am unable to do so.".

Personal Representative: In common law jurisdictions, a personal representative or legal personal representative is a person appointed by a court to administer the estate of another person, e.g. when a person dies without a Will.

POA (Power-of-Attorney): the authority to act for another person in specified or all legal or financial matters. A legal document giving power of attorney to someone.

Probate: *Probate* is the legal process whereby a Will is "proved" in a court and accepted as a valid public document that is the true last testament of the deceased.

Probate Attorney: A *probate lawyer* is a state licensed attorney who assists Personal Representatives and estate beneficiaries

Will: A **will** or **testament** is a legal document by which a person, the testator, expresses his or her wishes as to how his or her property is to be distributed at death, and names one or more persons, the executor, to manage the estate until its final distribution.

Photography Credits

Dreamstime.com   Treasure Map: page 5

Istock.com, Stock photo ID:589584162, William Potter, Will & Last Testament:page 8

Dreamstime.com, Brett Lamb, Roller Coaster: page 20

    <a href="https://www.dreamstime.com/stock-illustration-cartoon-rollercoaster-silhouette-amusement-park-image41884374#res 18211029">CartoonRollercoaster</a>

Dreamstime.com, Rallef, Advanced Medical Directive: page 23

    <a href="https://www.dreamstime.com/stock-photo-advanced-directive-image38080240#res18211029">Advanced directive</a>

Dreamstime.com, Everett Collection Inc., Ready for Adventure: page 28

    <ahref="https://www.dreamstime.com/stock-photo-ready-adventureimage52034180#res18211029">Ready for adventure</a>

Designed by Freepik, Person writing on a laptop: page 30

    <a href="http://www.freepik.com/free-photo/person-writing-on-a-laptop_992356.htm">

Courtesy of brittneiwashington.com, Three Steps of Healing, page 37

THANK YOU

Dear All who helped get this "out the door,"

It is with excitement and appreciation that I write this note. Please know you will receive a proper note in the mail, but I want to recognize each of you.

As my story was being written and I needed a boost in know-how, reinforcement or just a gentle word of advice, it would appear in short order as if by magic. Your interest became my encouragement to keep going; your suggestions – however kind – gave notice that some things needed "fixin!"

You are a dear group and I appreciate all of you tremendously. Thank you for helping my notes become a book.

From the bottom of my heart,

Mary Jane

Book Builders - Katrina Ayres, Owner, Positive Teaching Strategies, positiveteachingstrategies@gmail.com and Teresa Rodden, Author of *"Wholly Sober..."* www.Amazon.com.Wholly-Sober-Stopped-think-drinking : for your cheers, expectations and accountability!

Family - in particular, my son Sean: for his unfailing patience and very able assistance as my "secretary" in those critical first 10 days.

Forever friends and my neighbors - especially *The Robano and Fresh families:* for their ears, cheers and kindnesses.

Given, Ruth and Jim: for their time, their review and edits of this guide, their candid assessment and well-placed encouragement.

Noize, Veronika, Director of The DIY Marketing Center, www.DIYMarketingCenter.com : for her masterful marketing insights, direction and encouragement throughout this project.

Perkins, Priscilla, New England high school English teacher and NY forever friend: for her instant willingness to look at the final draft, making her structural edits in a quick, straight-forward style!

Scott, Dotty, Designer and Owner of Premium Websites **www.premiumwebsites.com**: for knowledge and assistance with my dpi and website!

Lastly, **Blazer, my Carolina Dog:** Thank you, "Boo," for happily taking all those walks to nowhere with me in all kinds of weather, while I worked it out one more time.

Made in the USA
Middletown, DE
11 September 2019